GUIDE FOR INTELLIGENT YOUNG POETS

Nathan Coppedge

THE PERPETUAL MOTION

GENIUS' GUIDE FOR

INTELLIGENT

YOUNG

POETS

Nathan Coppedge

INTRODUCTION

Nathan Coppedge

Poets, they say, can learn the
secret any year in their life.

Poets are born learners. They
prosper on life's complexities,
ideosyncracies, and raptures.

Born poets are blind to the
present, and omniscient about
the future.

Fateful poets --- one step
lower, and not very far --- keep
the keys to life's tragedy and
mystery. They are knowers of
beauty, unlike the ugliness of
the masters.

The genius of poetry is fertive,
not futile, and it is by following
the most universal patterns of
learning that the specific fruit
blooms upon the boughs of
lyrical knowledge.

Nathan Coppedge

GUIDE FOR POETS

Nathan Coppedge

ADVICE FOR POETS

COME OF LATE

**SURVIVE, LIVE, AND
STRIVE!**

Nathan Coppedge

BEYOND THE NOTIONS,

BEGIN TO THRIVE!

MAKE MANA YOUR DO-
MAIN

BUT DO NOT BE MANIC
WITH YOUR PEN---!

Nathan Coppedge

SAVE IT'S INK

DON'T LET IT SPLASH

**TURN TO WORDS THAT
DO NOT THRASH---!**

Nathan Coppedge

MEND IT'S WORK

AND CRITICAL REDS

MAKE TUNES BY MIND-
ING FORKS!

THE ROAD LEADS ON ---

Nathan Coppedge

IN TRAVELINGS OF
WORDS

THE SENTENCE OF THE
WRITER

BEGINS ITS MOODY
BRAWL ----

Nathan Coppedge

FORTUNES MADE OF FANTASIES

HEAVENS MINDING HELLS ----

Nathan Coppedge

THE TURN UPON THE PAGE ----

RESTS UPON ITS AGE ----

Nathan Coppedge

A CAPTIVATED REAC-
TION!

AND THE DUTIFUL
SCRIBE ----

CLEVERLY DESCRIBES ---

Nathan Coppedge

MOVING RHYTHMS'

RAPSODIZICAL PEPPER --- !

Nathan Coppedge

GATHER THESE SE-
CRETS

AND IT WILL MEND!

POETRY IS NOT DEAD!

TIME TO END !

Nathan Coppedge

GUIDE FOR INTELLIGENT YOUNG POETS

BIO

Nathan Coppedge has published three collections of poetry: Old Incantations, Poems by God, and Creeping Cadence. Nathan Coppedge is also previously the author of at least three other guides for intelligence (young adult's, children's, and baby's). Nathan also plans to write a guide for older adults focusing on immortality. Thus, if all poets seek immortality, the nature of his work is comprehensive.

www.ingramcontent.com/pod-product-compliance
Lightning Source LLC
Chambersburg PA
CBHW070247290526
45789CB00004B/1804